GREGORY L. VOGT

PLUTO

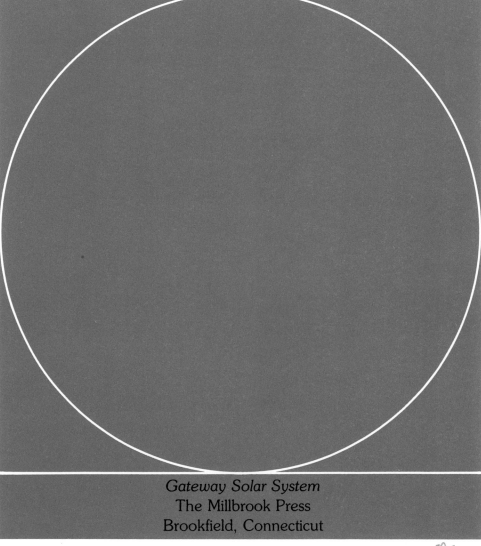

Gateway Solar System
The Millbrook Press
Brookfield, Connecticut

Published by The Millbrook Press
2 Old New Milford Road
Brookfield, Connecticut 06804

Library of Congress Cataloging-in-Publication Data

Vogt, Gregory.
Pluto / Gregory L. Vogt.
p.   cm.—(Gateway solar system)
Includes bibliographical references and index.
Summary: Presents information on Pluto, the farthest known planet,
and its moon, Charon. Includes a glossary and ''Pluto Quick Facts.''
ISBN 1-56294-393-6 (lib. bdg.)   ISBN 0-7613-0158-5 (pbk.)
1. Pluto (Planet)—Juvenile literature.   2. Project Mariner—
Juvenile literature.   [1. Pluto (Planet)] I. Title. II. Series:
Vogt, Gregory. Gateway solar system.
QB701.V64   1994
523.4'82—dc20   93-11224   CIP   AC

Photographs and illustrations courtesy of: National Aeronautics
and Space Administration: cover, pp. 4, 12, 16, 18, 20, 21, 23;
Lowell Observatory: pp. 7, 9; U.S. Naval Observatory: p. 14;
Pat Rawllings/SAIC: p. 25.

Solar system diagram by Anne Canevari Green

PLUTO

Clyde Tombaugh was born on an Illinois farm in 1906. Like many farm-raised children, he was likely to become a farmer when he grew up. But Clyde had other dreams. His uncle Lee had a small telescope, and he let Clyde look through it. Clyde saw moons circling Jupiter, and he saw the rings of Saturn. He also read his uncle's amateur astronomy book and memorized many of its pages.

Clyde did well in high school, but he had no money to go to college. When he was 20, he decided to build his own telescope. His first telescope was not very good, but the second one he built gave him beautiful views of the moon and planets.

Clyde made drawings of the surfaces of Mars and Jupiter and sent them to the Lowell Observatory in Flagstaff, Arizona. The director of the observatory wrote back and asked Clyde some questions. Eventually, Clyde was offered a job. When he boarded a train to Flagstaff in January of 1929 he had no idea that he would soon discover a new planet.

◄ Pluto appears as a thin, dim crescent in the light of the sun, more than 3.5 billion miles (5.6 billion kilometers) away.

At that time, *astronomers* (scientists who study objects in outer space) knew of only eight planets. The farthest known planet was Neptune. However, several astronomers, including Percival Lowell, founder of the Lowell Observatory, believed there was another planet.

Because of *gravity* (a force that causes objects to attract each other), all planets pull on each other, which changes the shape of their *orbits* (paths) around the sun. But the pull of all the known planets couldn't completely account for changes in the paths of orbit of Uranus and Neptune. Astronomers concluded there must be another planet in the solar system. This mystery planet must change the orbits of Uranus and Neptune, astronomers thought. Lowell predicted where to look for the mystery planet, nicknamed Planet X, but he died before it was found. The search fell to Clyde.

For many months, Clyde stayed up every clear night and took pictures of the stars. He would take one set of pictures and then, several nights later, take another set of pictures of the same sections of the sky. By comparing pictures of the same stars taken several days apart, he hoped to find the mystery planet.

Clyde was using a technique for planet searching called *parallax*. To understand what parallax is, hold up

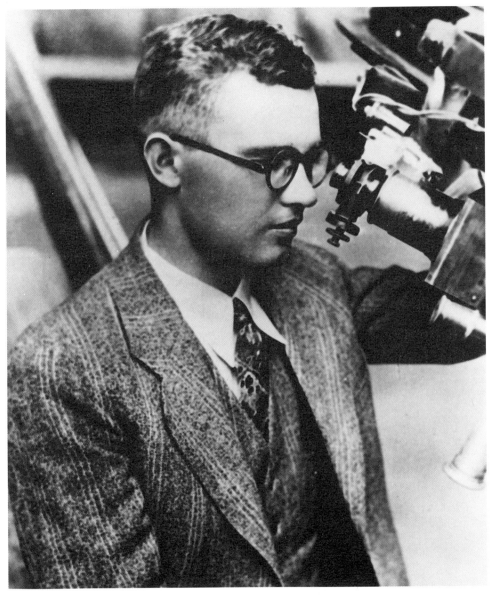

Young Clyde Tombaugh peers into the eyepiece of the Astrograph telescope at the Lowell Observatory.

one finger in front of your eyes and look at something far away. Open your right eye and close the left. Then, close your right eye and open the left. Your finger seems to jump from one side to the other! It will also seem to jump if you hold your finger at arm's length, but not as much. The farther away the object is, the smaller the jump. This appearance of movement when an object is viewed from different positions is known as parallax.

To search for a planet, astronomers use the technique of parallax by taking pictures of stars several days or more apart. Every day, Earth moves approximately 1.6 million miles (about 2.6 million kilometers) along its orbit in space. Looking at pictures taken six days apart is like having eyes 10 million miles (16 million kilometers) apart! Even so, stars are so far away from Earth that they take years to change positions in the sky. But planets, going around the sun, are much closer and can be seen to move in a few days.

Clyde searched many sky pictures and checked millions of stars before he found a very faint "star" in the constellation of Gemini that shifted a little more than one eighth of an inch (3.5 millimeters) in his photos. He made his discovery on February 18, 1930. The pictures that showed this shift were taken six days apart. The

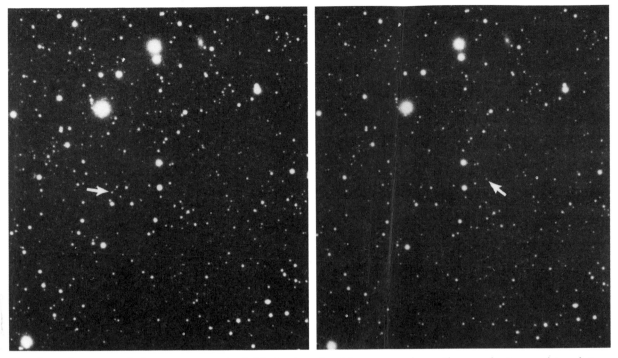

Tombaugh spotted the movement of Pluto (marked by arrows) on these photographic plates, taken six days apart.

small shift of the object indicated that it was close enough to be a planet, but at least a billion miles (1.6 billion kilometers) farther out from the sun than Neptune. Clyde Tombaugh had discovered Planet X very near the place in the sky where Percival Lowell had predicted it would be. The planet was eventually named Pluto and given the symbol of ♇, formed from initials of Percival Lowell.

The Most Distant Planet

It's easy to see why Pluto was so difficult to find. On a clear night, about 3,000 stars are visible to the naked eye. With a pair of binoculars to magnify starlight, about 200,000 stars become visible. With a medium-sized telescope, powerful enough to see Pluto, the number of stars you can see jumps to about 20 million. Until Clyde Tombaugh picked it out, Pluto looked just like millions of other faint stars.

Pluto has a very strange orbit. The orbits of all planets are in the shape of *ellipses*. (An ellipse is a somewhat flattened circle.) Therefore, as a planet orbits the sun, it is closer to the sun at some times than at others. This is true with Pluto as well. But Pluto's orbit is much more flattened than the others. (Only Mercury's orbit is almost as flat.) This means that Pluto, as it orbits the sun, ranges from as close as about 2,700 million miles (4,425 million kilometers) to as far away as about 4,500 million miles (7,375 million kilometers) from the sun. The difference between Pluto's closest point and its farthest is 1,800 million miles (2,950 million kilometers)!

Because Pluto's orbit is so flattened, it is not always the farthest planet from the sun. Pluto takes 248 Earth

Pluto

Neptune

Uranus

Saturn

Jupiter

Mars

Earth

Venus

Mercury

SUN

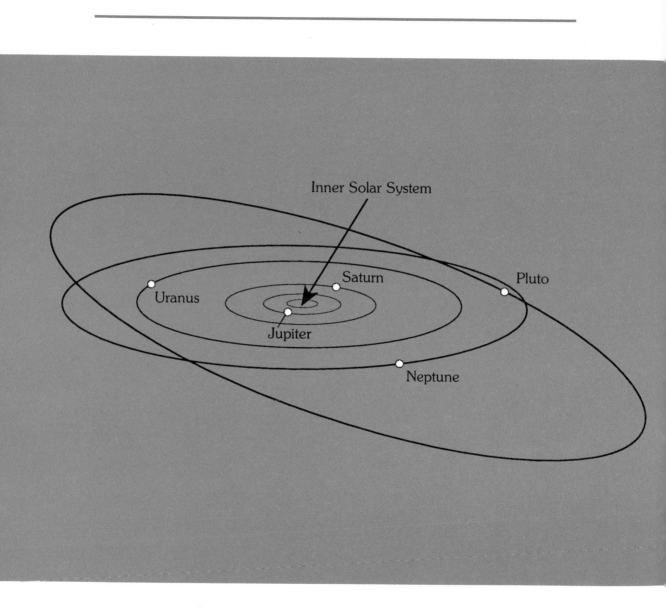

For periods during its orbit around the sun,
Pluto passes inside the orbit of Neptune.

years to make just one trip around the sun. Once in every orbit, Pluto gets so close to the sun that it dips within the orbit of the planet Neptune. For about 20 years, Neptune is the farthest planet from the sun. This is happening now. Neptune is farther from the sun than Pluto and will be until 1999, when Pluto crosses outside Neptune's orbit and heads back into deep space.

Because their orbits cross, some people have wondered if Pluto and Neptune are in danger of colliding. There isn't any chance of that happening because the angles of the planets' orbits prevent it. Even when Pluto is crossing Neptune's orbit, it is never closer than hundreds of millions of miles from Neptune.

A Double Planet

Even when viewed with the largest telescopes, Pluto is a very faint object. Yet careful study has yielded many interesting facts about this most distant neighbor to Earth. Pluto is a very small planet. It is only 1,420 miles (2,280 kilometers) in diameter. Seven moons in the solar system are larger than Pluto! Furthermore, Pluto is not alone. In 1978, astronomer James Christy noticed that pictures of Pluto showed a bulge in the planet. In several differ-

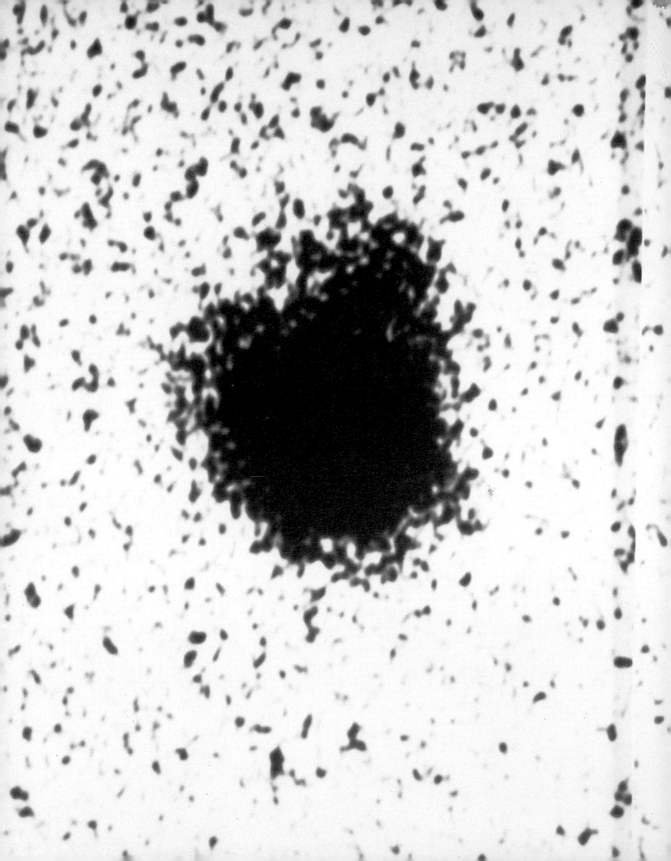

ent pictures Christy examined, the bulge appeared in different places. Christy concluded that Pluto had a moon. The moon was named Charon.

Christy realized that Charon was no ordinary moon. Earth's moon, about one quarter the diameter of Earth, orbits Earth at a distance of 238,000 miles (384,000 kilometers). Charon orbits Pluto at a distance of a mere 12,000 miles (about 20,000 kilometers)! Only the Martian moon Phobos orbits closer to its planet than Charon. But Phobos is more like an overgrown rock when compared to Charon.

Charon has a diameter of 732 miles (1,200 kilometers). It is nearly one half the diameter of Pluto. This makes Charon one of the largest moons in the solar system when compared to its planet. And because Charon is so close to Pluto, some astronomers call the two a *double planet.*

Their closeness links Pluto and Charon into a single rotation. Pluto spins on its axis once every 6.4 Earth days. Charon orbits Pluto in exactly the same time span.

◄ Astronomer James Christy first detected Pluto's moon, Charon, in this picture.

Like Earth's moon, Charon presents the same side of itself to Pluto at all times. (To see what this is like, invite an adult and a small child to join hands and spin around each other. Because the child is smaller than the adult, the child will make a larger circle around the adult as the adult makes a small circle. And while they are spinning, they will face each other.)

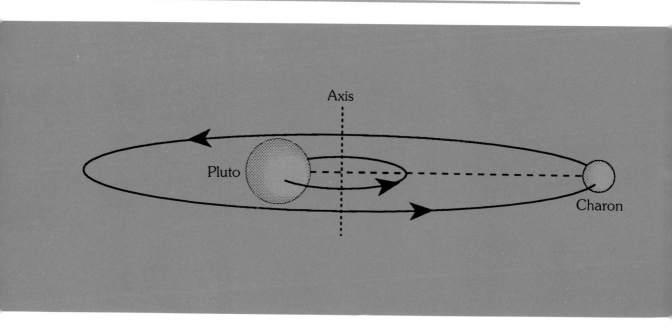

Pluto and Charon revolve around an imaginary axis, as if they were two ends of a twirling baton. Charon, the smaller of the two, has the larger orbit.

Ice Balls

Pluto and Charon appear to be made up mostly of water ice with rocky cores. At their great distance from the sun, they are never warmed enough by the sun's heat to melt. When Pluto is closest to the sun, the sun is still nearly 900 times fainter than it appears from Earth. When Pluto is farthest from the sun, the sun is more than 2,400 times fainter than it appears from Earth! This makes Pluto and Charon extremely cold, approximately 380 degrees below zero Fahrenheit (−230 degrees Celsius).

There is something strange about the surfaces of Pluto and Charon. Pluto's surface appears to be covered with frozen methane gas, while Charon's surface is covered with water ice. Charon's lesser gravity may have allowed the methane to escape while it was a gas, before it could freeze solid.

Another strange thing is that Pluto and Charon share an atmosphere. Because the two bodies are so close to each other, Pluto's atmosphere wraps around Charon as well. The atmosphere is very thin and consists of methane gas. This was discovered during a very rare event. In its motion around the sun, Pluto and Charon passed exactly in front of a very distant star. Astronomers on

board the National Aeronautics and Space Administration (NASA) Kuiper Airborne Observatory (a jet plane with a telescope) were ready for the event. They watched the star's brightness as Pluto and Charon passed in front of it. Instead of quickly blinking out the star's light, Pluto and Charon caused the star's light to fade before it blinked off. When no longer blocked, the star's light grew brighter again. This fading effect led the astronomers to conclude that Pluto and Charon had an atmosphere that was filtering the star's light.

Astronomers now think that Pluto and Charon's atmosphere is a temporary feature. When Pluto and Charon are nearest to the sun, the sun's heat (what little there is of it) warms the frozen methane on the surface of Pluto. Some of that methane turns into gas that becomes an atmosphere. Later, when Pluto and Charon travel farther from the sun, the methane refreezes on the surface of Pluto. The atmosphere doesn't reappear until Pluto and Charon are again near the sun, some 200 years later.

◀ From distant Pluto and Charon the sun appears small and faint.

The best picture of Pluto and Charon ever taken from Earth shows a pair of bright, blurry spheres. (The squares in the picture were produced by the camera.)

Pluto and Charon's Origin

One of the big questions about Pluto and Charon is where they came from. Many theories have been offered. One is that Pluto is an escaped moon of Neptune. Another is that Pluto is a fragment left by a great collision between large objects that took place during the formation of the solar system. Or Pluto may have been a leftover from the formation of the solar system.

Charon appears to have formed at a different time than Pluto. Somehow, Pluto and Charon ran into each other and remained together after the collision. One reason astronomers believe that a collision took place is that both Pluto and Charon are tipped sideways. That is, they rotate with their axes almost in the plane marked by Pluto's orbit, rather than almost at right angles to this

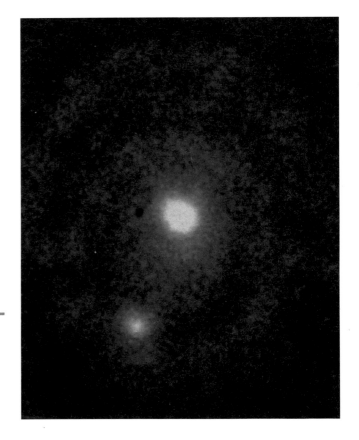

A far better picture was taken from above Earth's atmosphere by NASA's Hubble Space Telescope. The faint glow around the two spheres was caused by minor focusing problems.

plane, as many other planets do. Instead of having axes nearly up and down, the axes are sideways. A collision could account for this.

One thing astronomers lack is data from close-up observation to test their theories about Pluto and Charon. Just what are the surfaces like? Recent pictures from NASA's Hubble Space Telescope show that Pluto has a large, icy polar cap that is divided in half by a mysterious dark band. The pictures are not clear enough to show details, but there are shadowy bright and dark spots that could be broad basins or valleys. Pluto may also have large craters that were made by the impact of comets or asteroids.

Mission to Pluto

In 1962, NASA launched the *Mariner 2* spacecraft to the planet Venus. It was the first spacecraft to visit a planet and study it successfully. Since that first launch, NASA

Scientists used to believe that Neptune's moon Triton, shown in this picture ▶ taken by NASA's *Voyager 2* spacecraft, might be Pluto's twin. But new Hubble Space Telescope pictures of Pluto's surface show that Triton and Pluto may be very different.

has sent spacecraft to all of the planets in our solar system with one exception—Pluto. NASA hopes to add Pluto to the list early in the twenty-first century. Although still in the early planning stages, a mission to Pluto is likely to fly by the planet as early as the year 2006. While whizzing by, the spacecraft will take pictures of the planet and its moon and even test its atmosphere. Perhaps the spacecraft will provide enough information about the double planet for astronomers to decide where Pluto and Charon came from.

One More Mystery

Do you remember how the orbits of Neptune and Uranus provided a clue to the existence of Pluto? Because of irregularities in these orbits, astronomers concluded that a mysterious Planet X was pulling on them. But after Pluto was discovered, the mystery remained. Pluto turned out to be too small, with too little gravity, to completely account for the irregular orbits. This has led as-

An artist's view of a future spacecraft mission to Pluto and Charon. ▶

tronomers to think that Pluto may not be the last planet in our solar system. There may be another Planet X, perhaps even hundreds of Plutos, circling the sun in the farthest reaches of our solar system, waiting to be dis-covered.

PLUTO QUICK FACTS

Pluto: Named after the ancient Roman god of the underworld.

	Pluto	*Earth*
Average Distance from the Sun		
Millions of miles	3,596	93
Millions of kilometers	5,896	149.6
Revolution (one orbit around the sun)	247.68 Earth years	1 year
Average Orbital Speed		
Miles per second	2.89	18.6
Kilometers per second	4.74	30
Rotation (spinning once)	6 days, 9 hours, 18 minutes	24 hours
Diameter at Equator		
Miles	1,420	7,926
Kilometers	2,280	12,756
Surface Gravity (compared to Earth's)	0.06	1
Mass (the amount of matter contained in Pluto, compared to Earth)	0.002	1
Atmosphere	methane and other, unknown gas	nitrogen, oxygen
Satellites (moons)	1	1

Pluto's Moon	*Diameter*	*Distance From Planet*
Charon	732 mi 1,200 km	12,200 mi 20,000 km

27

GLOSSARY

Astronomer	A scientist who studies planets, moons, stars, and other objects in outer space.
Axis (plural: axes)	An imaginary line running through a planet from its north to its south pole.
Double planet	A nickname given to Pluto and Charon because of their nearness to each other and their closeness in size.
Ellipse	The shape of the orbital paths that planets follow around the sun.
Gravity	A force that causes all objects to attract each other.
Hubble Space Telescope	The orbiting observatory launched by NASA in 1990.
Kuiper Airborne Observatory	A NASA aircraft that carries a large telescope and other astronomical instruments.
Mariner 2	NASA's first successful interplanetary mission (to Venus in 1962).
Mass	The amount of matter contained in an object.
NASA	National Aeronautics and Space Administration.
Orbit	The path a planet takes to travel around the sun, or a moon to travel around a planet.
Parallax	The apparent shift that an object makes against a more distant background when it is viewed from different directions.
Revolution	One complete orbit of a planet around the sun, or a moon around a planet.
Rotation	The spinning of a planet or moon around its axis.
Satellite	A small body in space that orbits around a larger body. A satellite may be ''natural,'' as a moon, or ''artificial,'' as a spacecraft.

FOR FURTHER READING

Asimov, I. *Isaac Asimov's Library of the Universe, Pluto: A Double Planet?* Milwaukee, Wis.: Gareth Stevens Publishing, 1990.

Asimov, I. *How Did We Find Out About Pluto?* New York: Walker and Company, 1991.

NASA. *Our Solar System—A Geologic Snapshot,* NP 157. Washington, D.C.: National Aeronautics and Space Administration, 1991.

Tombaugh, C., and P. Moore. *Out of the Darkness—The Planet Pluto.* Harrisburg, Pa.: Stackpole Books, 1980.

ABOUT THE AUTHOR

Gregory L. Vogt works for NASA's Education Division at the Johnson Space Center in Houston, Texas. He works with astronauts in developing educational videos for schools.

Mr. Vogt previously served as executive director of the Discovery World Museum of Science, Economics, and Technology in Milwaukee, Wisconsin, and was an eighth-grade science teacher. He holds bachelor's and master's degrees in science from the University of Wisconsin at Milwaukee, as well as a doctorate in curriculum and instruction from Oklahoma State University.